Barbara Woodhouse

on

HOW YOUR DOG THINKS

RINGPRESS

RINGPRESS

Published by Ringpress Books Ltd,
Spirella House, Bridge Road,
Letchworth, Herts, SG6 4ET

Discounts available for bulk orders
Contact the Special Sales Manager at
the above address. Telephone (0462) 674177

First Published 1992
© 1992 MICHAEL CLAYDON WOODHOUSE

ISBN 0 948955 62 7

Printed and bound in Singapore
by Kyodo Printing Co

CONTENTS

FOREWORD

By Patrick Woodhouse

My mother was born in Ireland in 1910 at a boys' public school where her father was headmaster. Both her family and the boys at the school had a great many different animals and thus she grew up surrounded by them from a very early age. Dogs and other animals became so much a part of her life that it was obvious from the start that she would have animals around her all her life.

One of my earliest recollections of my mother was that she was always with one or other of her two dogs. In the early Fifties she had a Great Dane which responded so perfectly to her training that it won numerous prizes for obedience work. She realised that she really did have a gift for training dogs and she decided that she must use this gift to help others train their dogs.

She started professionally in 1951 with a dog training club meeting on Croxley Green, just a few yards from our house, which was called Campions. She soon had a class of 25-30 dogs and their owners every Sunday and this led to the founding of four other training clubs, in nearby towns, which were always full of dog owners wishing to learn. Her weekends and evenings were thus spent doing the thing she enjoyed most, the training of dogs.

Her own Great Danes, Juno and Junia, were trained to such a high standard that they could work in films and on TV programmes by just being shown the action. Then, by simply giving them a command or signal, they would act out the part to perfection. Juno, mother's best known Great Dane, became known as " Take 1 Juno" on the sets of the studios where she worked with famous actors like Sir Alec Guinness, Clark Gable, Roger Moore, Eric Morecambe, and many others. Her Great Danes acted in more than eighty TV and movie productions in their careers, and many of the films were produced by my mother and often directed by her as well.

Her career really started to take off when she was invited to do a TV series about dog training for the BBC and the series was to be called: Training Dogs The Woodhouse Way. This series became such a success that it was repeated three times during its first year and led to two more series and a host of appearances on other programmes in which she was interviewed and in which she demonstrated her methods of dog training to TV stars such as Terry Wogan and Michael Parkinson. In the United States the programmes of her dog training became so popular that they are still being shown to this very day. She became known as the "Dog Lady" and her books became some of the best-sellers ever known in America. In 1980 she won the cherished TV award presented by the Pye Corporation as the Female TV Personality Of The Year and went on to win the title of the World's Best Dog Trainer. Since those hectic days she has travelled the world demonstrating her methods to countless dog owners and visiting numerous countries, including the United States of America, Canada, Australia, New Zealand, Singapore and many parts of Europe, before her death in 1988 following a stroke.

I hope that you, the reader, will get a great deal of help from this book and that it will answer all your questions about the difficulties many people experience when training their dogs. I am sure that the sense of achievement you will experience when you have successfully trained your dog to do even the simplest of exercises will give you a sense of oneness with your dog that cannot be bettered by a relationship with any other animal. May I wish you every success with your training and hope that your dog will become, to quote my mother: "A DOG THAT IS A PLEASURE TO ALL AND A NUISANCE TO NO ONE."

If you want to communicate with animals, you must have an intense love of them, says Barbara Woodhouse.

INTRODUCTION

I believe that animals have been talking to human beings ever since we were all made and put into this world 'for mutual society, help, and comfort, both in prosperity and adversity', to quote from the marriage service; and that if we human beings have been unbelievably slow in taking advantage of the gifts we have been offered, we have nobody but ourselves to blame. And I feel that, as animals are so much quicker in picking up our thoughts and words than we are in picking up theirs, they must have a very poor opinion of the intelligence of the human race.

This is not to deny that in every race and in every age there have always been individuals known for their love and understanding of the animal kingdom, who have forged indestructible bonds of friendship with the animal world. Most of us have read, with absorbed interest, of people like Tom Faggus and his strawberry mare, or Prince Llewellyn whose faith in his dog failed him in a crisis. Practically everyone knows of someone who has a 'way with animals' and who seems able to communicate moods, notions and sympathies, with or without using words, to animal friends. Those people are indeed blessed, their lives are a fulfilment and an example of what we would like to see happening among the human races. But I fear that with human beings the hates of the many overcome the love of the few. So few animals hate, and so many millions of them wait to give to someone or other the love and submission they long to show to a master!

How is it possible to learn how to talk to animals? I think one has to have an intense love of them, and an inborn conviction that they are eager to comply with our wishes, if we can just show them how. Looking back, it seems to me that there has never in my life been a misunderstanding with an animal that has not been capable of being straightened out for our mutual well being. So much of my communication with animals is wordless, words as such meaning nothing to animals, but being simply carriers of tone. It is our way of employing words that matters. We could use the same words to praise, to scold, to encourage, and to excite, if we had enough command of our intonations to make each usage different; but how many people can do this? Very few. Therefore, in their contact with animals many have to try to teach them the actual meanings of words, and this must of necessity be a very slow business.

Patience is a vital quality in dealing with animals: lose your temper with an animal and you have built up a barrier that will have to be slowly broken down again before mutual trust and confidence is restored. But I do not mean by this that one should never give the impression of having lost one's temper, for I firmly believe that occasionally an animal has to be very severely spoken to for misbehaviour, but that the severity must be 'put on'. It must not be a genuinely lost temper. When you put it on, you can take it off again, and bring back the loving tone immediately; the animal knows the difference and is ready and waiting to be loved again should he mend his ways.

Animals often 'play up' their owners. One so often sees lapdogs which are completely impervious to honeyed talk, but which respond immediately to sensible commands. There are few animals that cannot distinguish the sharp edge on the usually placid voice which reminds them that it is, at that moment, better to obey. I do not believe that all animals are born good, nor do I believe that one can reform all wrongdoers. As in the human race, we have rogues, and unless one has endless time to spend on these rogues perhaps one would be better engaged in teaching the right-minded animals. However, I personally love the bad animals. They are a challenge to my spirit, and if I had the time I would concentrate a great deal more on the rogues. The animals that need my help and sympathy are the frightened ones, the misunderstood ones, the ones with the wrong owners, and the bad ones. But to carry out this work would mean separating most of the animals from their owners and never returning them, for in nine cases out of ten it is the human being who is at fault. So, when readers first try talking to animals I advocate confining their activities to the normal animals, sound in heart and mind, leaving a few of us only to deal with the really bad ones.

Chapter One

THE OWNER

There must be few people who have never owned a dog at some time or other in their lives, not necessarily a dog belonging exclusively to themselves, but one shared with the family. The main reasons for owning or sharing a dog come under these three headings in my opinion: for pleasure, profit or protection. I believe by far the greatest number are owned purely and simply for the joy of having a dog either to play with if you are young, or to take for walks and keep you fit if you are not so young, or just for the sheer delight of having a lovely creature round the house to be admired, to admire you, and to keep you company. In this book we are going to exclude those dogs that are kept for profit, as stock-in-trade of a business which must succeed or fail through the amount of money made; the business man or woman presumably sees to it that their dogs are made as attractive as possible to would-be purchasers. If the animals are fierce or unkempt they will not find buyers easily. So we will presume that they are sold before the disobedience, if it exists, has had time to develop or show itself. We are solely concerned with the dog that belongs to the ordinary man in the street.

I wonder how many owners think about the responsibilities of dog ownership before they go out and buy a cuddly little puppy? Too few, I fear. A dog does not need palatial surroundings, but its basic needs must be catered for. It must have an adequate diet, it must be exercised, and kept clean. If the dog becomes ill the owner must nurse the dog, administering medicines, and perhaps holding the dog while the vet gives an injection. The mental outlook of the owner towards these operations is very important, for the dog at once picks up its owner's nervous reactions; and people who turn a ghastly white when anything has to be done to their dogs are not the ones to hold them for the vet. The dog senses their nervousness and becomes terrified at once. They should try to get a less squeamish member of the family to help.

I find one of the most troublesome things to persuade your dog to accept is that he may be caressed in the street by

A big dog like a Great Dane attracts attention wherever it goes.

all and sundry. My dog, being a Great Dane, attracts attention wherever she goes. She is just the right height for everyone to stroke without bending down. Therefore, as one cannot stop dog lovers caressing dogs (or baby lovers kissing babies) one has to train the dog to put up with it without showing annoyance or trying to be too friendly. It is always extremely annoying when you have a trained dog, and have put it to the 'sit' or 'down' outside a shop, to come and find a crowd round it trying to make it get up and talk to them, or trying to feed it on everything from a lollipop to a mince pie. When one's dog is trained fully, it must of course refuse food of all sorts from anyone but its owner or owners. Otherwise there is always the risk that a burglar or some malicious person may poison it. On the other hand there is the risk that a dog so trained, on going to kennels while its owner is away, may refuse food. This has happened and has been extremely worrying for the people concerned. I think if you are likely to leave your dog a lot with strangers, it is best not to teach it to refuse food from other people. I have found occasionally that my dog has had to take food whilst acting in a film, from people other than myself, and I have only had to introduce the person who is to give her food, and tell her it's all right, for her to take the food willingly. But I do not think many of my readers will at this stage have achieved, or perhaps ever will, such perfect communication as I have with my dog. For if they have reached that stage of training they will probably not have bought this book.

There are a number of bad habits which dogs can get into, which cause a lot of heartache for their owners. There are the boisterous dogs who jump up on greeting their owners, or visitors to the house, or even people in the street. There are dogs that chew up everything in the house, and which one daren't leave alone a minute in a room without finding there is no longer a newspaper to read, or your slippers to wear. Then there are the dogs who bark incessantly at everyone or anything, or the dogs that welcome everyone as though he were a long-lost friend, and won't bark at all. There are dogs that chase cats or other livestock; dogs that chase cars and bite postmen; horrid dogs that bite their owners; dogs that are only seen at mealtimes or when they want to be let into the house to sleep. There are the dogs that soil the whole house when they feel like it, and who have therefore to be kept outside for health reasons, as no one should tolerate in the house a dog that is not house trained. Then there are the dogs that are so clean and well trained that they will not relieve themselves when away from home. I once had a Great Dane like that, and it worried me terribly. I spent one day at the seaside taking her for miles trying to find a suitable piece of grass which she would use. There are the dogs that jump on all the furniture, and refuse to come off. And there are the dogs that steal food, so that one has to be always on the alert not to put a bit of food within their reach. Lastly there are the dogs that won't come when they are called and the dogs that fight all other dogs, so that it is a misery to take them out. I would like to say that in my opinion if, by the time you have owned a dog six months he has any of the faults I have listed, except nerves, it is in

A dog must learn to respect its owner, and to obey all commands without question.

practically every case your own fault. You have not really persisted in training your dog in the right way. I meet an enormous number of dog owners in a year at my courses, and hundreds of others whom I never meet write to me from all over the country for help or advice with the training of their dogs. I am always ready to admit there may be a dog somewhere that is untrainable, but it is a rare exception.

But that is more than I can say of dog owners. There are hundreds of dog owners everywhere who ought never to keep a dog. These are some of the reasons why. They believe that by giving dog everything he wants he will repay their kindness by implicit obedience and love. That is nonsense. A dog must respect his owner from the day he joins the household. Occasionally in every dog's life there comes a time when firmness is a necessity. If at that time the owner only tries coaxing, the dog will become the master, and the true understanding which exists between the master and dog has been lost. There are plenty of owners who think that it is cruel to control their dog in any way. They really believe that for a dog to be happy he must have complete freedom to go where he will when he will. I have even heard dog owners tell me, not very logically, that it is my duty to put my beloved bitch into kennels when she is on heat so that their dog will not be attracted round to my home when fights and other troubles might develop. The idea that they might control their own dog's movements, and leave my bitch safely in my own home and garden, never enters their heads. To impress their duty on them I have often taken their dogs, unwelcome on my premises,

to the police station, and they have had to fetch them and pay for their keep.

Another erroneous notion is that a dog is only happy when racing over the countryside chasing rabbits or livestock, and that he must not be thwarted by being called home. The numbers of times I have heard owners telling me it took two hours to catch their dog is unbelievable. These dogs neither love nor respect their owners. A dog that loves its owner cannot bear him or her out of sight or hearing, and will not run off for hours on his own private concerns. Sometimes harsh things have to be done with dogs who are out of control. At these times the mind of the owner should try not to send out waves of horror, nor to think, 'I can't stand this, I shall take my dog home,' for soon the stormy scene will become a placid one and the dog taught for life that respect is necessary for true happiness. Rushing from one training school to another only bewilders the dog, for every trainer has his own tried methods and is unlikely to be impressed or influenced by other ways that the owner may have been taught. Most trainers recognise that their pupils have been to another school so they shouldn't try and deny it, for dog trainers have long ago learnt that absolute honesty in dealing with dogs is essential; if the owner is a bit of a 'story-teller', her dog will not be the easiest to train.

Many owners think a dog should eat until he can eat no more and that it is cruel to give their dogs only the correct amount of food, however much those lovely eyes plead. There are excellent books dealing with the nutrition of dogs, and most dog food manufacturers are only too pleased to tell owners about feeding, so I shall not enlarge on the theme beyond saying that it is not cruel to diet your dog. He will not be too fat, and therefore lazy, when you wish to take him for a long ramble, and lastly he will cost less to keep when given his suitable rations. I do believe that dogs need extra vitamins and that the ordinary diet they get does not always provide all they need. Vitamins A and B are, in my opinion, the ones they seem to need, in most cases, as supplement.

There are thousands of dog owners whose lives are made a misery by their male dogs' insistence on stopping at every lamp post. This is a thing I never allow. A dog of mine would get his freedom whenever possible and at this time he relieves himself as often as he wishes, but I should get extremely annoyed if I were forcibly stopped by my dog in a walk through the streets, and I should be tempted to commit murder if my dog attempted to relieve himself on a shop front or near anyone's front door. I am revolted by the way dog owners allow this disgusting behaviour. I have dogs brought to my classes who try this on. They are only warned twice and then they are removed from the class. This does not mean that I cannot forgive a puppy or a nervous dog for forgetting himself, it means that an adult dog whose owner is not attending properly to his behaviour, and allows him to soil our hall, will be sent out. Each session only lasts two and a half hours, and any dog can behave himself for that time. If not, the owner is at liberty to take him out for exercise. Most owners think this lamp post stopping is natural and must be allowed. I wonder whether they do or do not train their children? I look

upon dogs as having the same mental capacity as children of five years old, and I think a dog or a child of that age should be trained to cleanliness. And as for dog owners who say that they must put everything out of reach of their dogs, so that it shall not be torn up, and who blame themselves if something does get destroyed because they didn't remember to put it away, I can only assume that they have little else to do. In my busy life, I certainly haven't time to be so careful.

Let us for a few moments analyse the owners of these misfits, and see if we can tackle the problem by re-educating the owners. Without a moment's hesitation I say: 'Yes we can'. If the owners are interested enough and fond enough of their dogs to read training books or to attend training schools or courses, they are well worth the time spent in helping them. For the most part those who seek my help and advice are women. The female of the species undoubtedly not only wields the rolling pin, but holds the dog's lead as well. Older children I find make excellent handlers of dogs, but owing to school they seldom have sufficient time to be entrusted with the entire training of the dog, so it naturally falls to Mother.

The worst dog trainers are undoubtedly mothers with young children; they simply haven't time or energy to give to an animal. The result is the dog becomes a nuisance. He is regarded as the plaything of the children, and seldom have the children been taught to respect the privacy of the dog. It amazes me what patience most dogs show towards children. They suffer being dressed up and put in a pram, they endure their ears being pulled, and being hugged too tightly, and they endure being woken up when they want to sleep in the gentle manner of nice dogs. But I am definitely not in agreement with people who buy puppies for small children, and then abandon the puppy to the mercy of the children and feel angry if the puppy bites the children or tears up their things. Few children would stand what many puppies have to put up with, and if in time the puppy grows adult and no longer wishes to be the target for little Willie's tantrums, and answers back with a bite, it is always the dog that is to blame, never the child. I can quite honestly say that when my children were tiny I never left my dogs to play with them unsupervised in case, without meaning to be unkind, the child did something that hurt or annoyed the dog. The children were trained to 'let sleeping dogs lie', and that they must not approach a dog that was not wagging its tail happily.

Most dogs seem to put up with the rough handling children give them in the same way as they put up with the nips from their own puppies. But without growling, how can a dog show he has had enough? That is why I think all small irresponsible children should be supervised in their play with dogs. Once the dog has learnt that only by growling can he check the children and their unwanted attentions, it is a short step to the quick irritable bite, and a very short step to becoming a problem dog or one on his last walk to the vet. Children must be trained if they are to be good companions to dogs, and that is the way round I think it should be, for the human being always has the advantage over the dog, as it is the human being who decides his destiny. I have with my own eyes seen boys and girls send their dogs after livestock. How then is the dog to know that to chase cats and chickens, not to mention sheep, is a crime? Children can quickly learn to train their small dog to quite a high standard of obedience, and love doing it. If they have a pride and personal interest in the dog they will not teach him bad ways. It is up to the parents to see this interest is cultivated.

How many grown-ups make suitable handlers? I regretfully say good handlers are few and far between, the main reason being lack of light and shade in their personal character and make-up. Every day of my life I am astounded at the amount of annoyance and inconvenience owners put up with on account of their dogs. And by this I do not mean having holidays restricted by not being able to take their dog along, nor the work resulting from polished floors being covered with paw marks. I mean real good cases of having their new linoleum torn to shreds, or the baker refusing to call because the dog bites him, or not being able to turn over in bed at night because the dog bites if disturbed from his position in the centre of the bed; or not being able to knit one's husband a pullover, because the dog dislikes his mistress knitting and bites her as soon as the knitting is picked up! Or having to watch a dog chew something up because he won't let go. Or having to stay rigid in the garage because your guard dog has misunderstood whom to guard! These and countless other faults are borne by countless owners for no other reason than that they love their dogs. I feel very humble when I read their letters, for I

Children can make first-class handlers, but they must be trained to understand how a dog's mind works.

doubt whether I would tolerate these faults so easily. On the other hand I get irritable with the people who try to persuade me to take their dogs from them and train them myself, for I explain that if I trained their dog it would probably take me half a day to get him trained to quite a high standard; but that the dog would return to them just as bad as ever, because they themselves would not be trained in controlling him, and that it is their voice and their manner of working the dog that matters.

Chapter Two

THE MIND OF THE DOG

The thing that has always struck me forcibly is how awful it must be to be a dog. You don't choose the home you live in, nor the owner. If you want to leave it, you run away or commit crimes for which you get punished. If you run away you are either taken back to the same unsavoury home or given away to one that may prove just as horrid or, if not claimed or found another home, your short life on this earth may be ended for you by the police or a welfare society. You can't argue with your owner except by refusing to carry out commands or, in worse cases, biting the person you disagree with. You can't speak, so a psychiatrist can't help you. The vet only examines you and gives an opinion as to your state of health. A trainer may or may not understand you and for brief moments give you supreme happiness or dejected hopelessness. Yet with all the troubles in the world you are always ready to give unbounding love and affection to those to whom you belong, if only they will understand you. You can read the mind of your owner and all with whom you come in contact, yet your simplest wants are often misunderstood by humans.

You are always interested in things like smells which human beings seem to totally disregard and, if a certain smell particularly interests you so that you don't even hear your owner calling, you will have a cross owner. You get left behind suddenly in a strange boarding kennel with people you may not know or like, and a multitude of other dogs who are also bewildered by the action of their owners. You show how upset you were when they do eventually come and fetch you by an overpowering welcome, yet the same thing happens again and the owners seem to completely misunderstand your dread of being deserted. Weeks before they leave you, you have picked up by telepathy the unrest in the household as the time approaches for their departure, and you know you are to be left once more with strangers, with no assurance that you will ever see your owners again. You are encouraged to defend your home, yet, if you defend it too well and bite that nasty-looking man in a black hat who swaggers up the drive, you are

A dog is prepared to give unbounding love and affection, even when it is often misunderstood by its owner.

punished for biting and probably shut up somewhere. How were you to know which people needed biting and which people just needed frightening?

After all, dogs were really meant to live natural lives whereby they probably ran at least twenty miles per day in pursuit of food. Their instincts were highly developed to gauge by scent alone the approach of danger, and their lives were fraught with risk of sudden death. Now most of that is passed. The sniffing of a lamp post by a male dog not inoculated against Leptospirosis is far more likely to cause quick death than murder by another animal or human being. No longer can a dog wander off and fight to annex a wife for himself by sheer force of superior masculinity. He is expected to behave at all times like a gentleman and ignore the calls of nature. Do you wonder sometimes his mind gets a bit disturbed? He doesn't always fit into flat life in Kensington. I think dogs on the whole are very accommodating creatures. They love human companionship, and endure hours of boredom in the hope that a walk or a game will come their way. They endure beauty treatment that in the past no self-respecting dog would have endured. They have to eat what is given to them instead of pouncing on the nearest sheep and gorging their tummies. And cats mustn't be chased? In return for all this they get a warm comfortable home, vitaminised food of the right quality to ensure all their vital organs are sustained and nourished. They get as much exercise as the health and desire of their owner permits. They sometimes get unrestricted romps with interesting dogs and, if their owners are sensible, they learn their lessons like human children. Sometimes they get too little affection; often they get overwhelming affection which has exactly the opposite effect on a dog's mind to that the owner thinks it will have. Occasionally unfortunate dogs get only hatred, misunderstanding and despair for a bedfellow.

The mind of a dog is really very simple to understand. All he wants is someone to love and respect, a reasonable amount of fun, to be useful to his owner and to have a comfortable well-fed tummy. At certain times his mind runs almost exclusively on sex, then it is not easily controlled by the owner. On the whole, the life of the dog and owner have to be in tune to get perfection out of the partnership. Both must respect each other's likes and dislikes, and a deep understanding must exist between them. What governs the behaviour of a dog? How far does his mind think? What can be put down to instinct? I think that, before the puppy is eight weeks old, instinct is nearly ninety-nine per cent of the dog's mind, and the control of his actions is almost entirely guided by the desire to eat, sleep, keep warm and play. After that the human contacts he makes, the discipline he receives, and the affection he develops for the person who nurtures him, begin to play an

important part in the forming of the dog's mind and character. No two people are alike, no two dogs are alike. We often see in the same litter an entirely different make-up in character and looks. Although it helps to study pedigrees and see the parents of the dog you are going to take into your home, it is no guarantee that the dog will be anything like the last dog you had with similar breeding, or even like the rest of the litter he was born into. This is where owners trip up badly. They feel 'done in the eye' if the breed that was previously a joy to them lets them down. They assume, for example, that all Border Collies are easily trained, affectionate and nice to own. They get extremely annoyed if their small puppy bites them, or won't come when called, and maybe is dirty in the house, when their previous one made none of these mistakes. From that moment the dog hasn't quite the same loving owner as he had when he was purchased, and he subconsciously picks up the irritation of his owner by telepathy. He becomes aggressive because the owner is not feeling too well disposed towards him, and a vicious circle is started in more senses than one.

To train a dog with sympathy and understanding one must try to understand a dog's mind. That mind has several big thoughts, his body a few major requirements. Firstly, the body governs the mind to a great extent when the puppy is young. The need to eat, sleep, urinate and defecate are the main factors. It hasn't entered a dog's mind that it is wrong to puddle on the floor or soil his bed. His reactions are entirely spontaneous. When scolded for these things he does not at first connect

Showing love is of paramount importance when training a dog, even if you have to be very firm in the initial stages in order to achieve basic obedience.

his action with the cross words and 'fear' enters his mind. Nature's reactions to fear are many: some animals crouch and stay as still as if dead; others snarl and attack the thing or person that frightens them; others turn on their tummy believing this age-old action of a baby animal will help them; some urinate and open their bowels with seemingly no control whatsoever. Most young animals rush to drink from their mothers if frightened. In training dogs we must take all these things into consideration before we punish a dog and look upon him with disappointment or disgust.

Only by repetition do dogs know what is right or wrong when very tiny. Their minds cannot reason what is right or wrong. They learn from experience of the tone of voice of the owner, or the resulting jerk on a choke chain, or by being put into their kennels when naughty or any other punishment that the owner has thought to be suitable. But whatever the punishment, it is not always effective, for one has to gauge the natural reaction of the dog's mind to the treatment he is receiving or is about to receive. In many instances this reaction is to bite the person that is reproving him or to lick and jump up on the person who is praising him. That is why, in my school, I am very loathe to correct a keen and loving dog from jumping up in the early stage of training, for, if you repress its natural exuberance and show of affection in the only way the dog knows, you may also be inhibiting the dog's natural love for you.

I think this love is of paramount importance and I constantly hug, kiss and play joyfully with my pupils even if I have had to be extremely firm with them to achieve initial obedience. The result is that there enters the dog's mind a memory of affection and fun rather than fear of correction. For, make no mistake, dogs don't object to fair correction. In fact, if you face up to it, the most loving dogs often seem to belong to owners to whom one would hate to be related in any way. A dog longs for love and he thinks that by fawning on a horrid owner he may achieve his desire, and so keeps on fawning ad infinitum. But woe betide the owner who refuses to face up to the fact that a dog's mind is not a human mind, and firmly believes that any correction given to the dog will be remembered by that dog for ever and held against the owner.

The dog has an enviable mind; it remembers the nice things in life and quickly blots out the nasty. That is why, when people tell me their small puppy was attacked by a big dog and that in later life made him into a fighter, I say, 'Bunkum! ' If your dog wasn't a fighter by nature, he wouldn't be one. Forget the past and deal with the present. Face up to the fact that his hormone balance or his hereditary characteristics are far more likely to make him into a fighter than having been attacked by another dog. After all, in the wild state, dogs were always attacking each other, and even play amongst dogs consists of biting and knocking each other over. Lack of firmness and leadership by the owner is far more likely to cause emotional upsets in the dog than a previous attack by another dog. Dogs are no different to human beings in the wide range of characteristics and temperaments they possess. Dogs can have nervous breakdowns the same as human beings but dogs get typed as bad-tempered or disobedient. Few people think of the stresses of modern life, the noise of the traffic, the perpetual human rat race which spills off on to the dog as his owner is forever dashing out of the front door leaving the dog behind bewildered. The slower ordered life of the past has almost disappeared for dogs and owners, and dogs get put to sleep for things which could easily be cured, if only the owners would understand them and give them time.

Chapter Three

INSTINCTIVE BEHAVIOUR

The meaning of instinct given in a dictionary is: "The natural impulse apparently independent of reason or experience by which animals are guided." To me, this sounds very sensible. Take a puppy: every time he is asked to do something he doesn't want to do, or if he fears the approach of a bigger or fiercer dog than himself, he quickly lies on the floor with his legs in the air and his tummy exposed to the enemy. This attitude has come down through generations of domesticated dogs; yet it is the remains of an instinct in the wild. For in the wild no young puppy would have been attacked in this position; it was against the laws of nature. This habit is a great hindrance in training, for when you try to put a dog's lead on, he just waves his legs in the air and bites, especially if you try to get hold of his collar. Therefore we must train these dogs that this position will not save them from being made to do what we wish them to do, and in fact, I jerk them very quickly into the upright position if they try it on.

I think dogs are guided a lot by instinct, but a lot more by smell, and I think the smell can alter considerably from human to human according to the attitude of the human being. For example, why is it that dogs take instantly to some people and won't go near others, especially when those they dislike want to be friends with them? I think each human being has a friendly or unfriendly smell which dogs can always detect. Fear, I believe, sends out an unpleasant smell as far as humans are concerned, for dogs sense nervous people yards away. Why do dogs go and sniff at the base of another dog's tail? It is the old instinct to find out whether the dog belongs to his pack or another by the scent from the anal glands. Why do dogs roll in something dirty, in spite of knowing quite well they will get beaten or bathed for their sin? Because in the old times of wild dogs they wanted to show their enemies they were about by leaving their own scent on something not carrying it. That is also why they lift their legs where any other dog has lifted his leg, rather like a game of beggar my neighbour. The dog's particular scent indicates to his pack where he has gone.

A dog must do all that it is told, provided the thing it is asked to do is fair and reasonable.

Certainly one cannot give in to instinct when training a dog to be obedient. A dog must do what he is told without question, provided the thing he is asked to do is fair and reasonable. I do not think jumping through fire is fair or reasonable, and I hate to see animals made to do it as a trick. Animals have an instinctive fear of fire from the old days of forest fires, and to train them to do this trick must, in my opinion, need a certain amount of cruelty. Wherever possible we use the dog's natural instincts if they can be guided into the right channels. Take tracking, for example. A dog's natural instinct is to find food by using his nose, and I think most trainers agree that food at the end of the trail is the great incentive when teaching a dog to track; that is how I train anyway. The more highly-bred, the less instinct a dog possesses, in my opinion. The stray mongrel reverts to type very often, only coming out to hunt for food when it is night time, and snapping at anyone who tries to catch him. That is the ancient instinct to stay free, and I feel that if there were stray bitches about at the same time, that particular dog would soon have a pack living with him. The old instinct of turning round and round, making a hole in the ground to sleep in still persists in the domestic dog today. Most of them turn round two or three times before settling down to sleep, yet they don't make the floor more comfortable by doing so. The old instinct of bone-burying for future consumption still remains strong in our dogs, although they hardly ever remember where they have buried them, as they are not usually hungry enough. It takes training to make a dog stop digging up the

garden to bury his bones, but it can be done.

Everyone who has a lot to do with the training of dogs can't help but notice that bitches are far easier to train than dogs. The reason is that, except when she is 'on heat' or in the throes of a 'pseudo pregnancy,' a bitch's attention is not disturbed by matters of sex – although Greyhounds are not raced within three months after being on heat, because they are supposed not to be at their best at those times. A bitch is better tempered than a male dog on the whole, for the fighting instinct for supremacy over other dogs is not so prevalent, although bitches do get extremely jealous, especially of their own offspring. I have known mother and daughter fight incessantly so that one has to be parted with. This often happens in the human race – mother and daughter don't get on – so it is nothing new to us to find it in the animal kingdom as well. Sex is a thing no so-called psychiatrist can fathom, for the dog again cannot answer questions as to whether his sex life is normal, or whether he had unpleasant sexual adventures when young. Therefore the dog owner must rely on experience of sexual behaviour in dogs and use that knowledge to make the dog's existence healthy and happy.

Many dogs literally seem to have minds that rely almost entirely on sex for most of their lives, and these oversexed dogs are a curse to themselves and their owners; they are abnormal and should not, in my opinion, perpetuate the race, for in these days of built-up areas and lack of free run for dogs an oversexed dog is a curse. You can't get through to their minds at all without intensive training for long periods and with a greater degree of firmness than, in my opinion, is kind. I say with all my heart that, unless the owner of this dog particularly requires him for show purposes, the dog should be 'doctored' to make his life happy and that of his owners equally trouble-free. Wild cries of: 'I shouldn't like to do that to my dog,' or, 'I would hate to take his nature away,' are bound to be heard from ignorant people who don't know enough about castration, whose vets have little or no personal experience of it or from people who know someone who knows someone who had their dog done and the dog got fat and dull. What they didn't bother to find out was, what was the owner of the castrated dog like? Did that owner feed the dog every time he asked for food? Did they reduce the food that they had been giving the dog, as he was no longer using up energy fussing over sex matters? Did they give it reasonable exercise and sufficient training to make his life interesting? These are the factors that make a castrated dog no different to any other dog except that he is happier in every way and a joy to own in town or country, with or without other dogs. Only when sex is a nuisance need this be done, and I heartily recommend it to everyone, whatever the age of the oversexed dog.

What goes on in the mind of the oversexed male dog? The answer is, nothing but the desire to copulate. It doesn't really matter whether the bitch he meets is on heat, it often doesn't matter whether the dog he meets is male or female, he is quite happy to carry out his sexual exercises on the leg of a child or even the furniture. He growls ferociously at other dogs, willing to fight any of them due to nervous sexual excitement; he often bites his owner in a fit of frustration. He barks or whines most of the day and cannot at any time be made to attend with proper concentration when there are other dogs about, whatever their sex. Many people think they will cure this oversexed menace by letting him 'have a bitch'. How sorry they will be if they do this! All the full flood of sexual fulfilment makes the dog become a maniac, for now his instincts are more fully aroused than ever and discipline becomes more impossible than ever. Yet get this dog alone in some place where no dog has been, and no smells or dogs are about, and he will often be the nicest possible dog, gay, loving and obedient.

Why then are owners so queer about castrating dogs? I have had more than 400 dogs done on my advice, and in every case the owner and dog are happy where formerly the dog was impossible, the owner fed-up, and the partnership in grave danger of being ended. But these owners are taking my advice as to diet of a strict nature and are continuing the training of the dog, for castration takes time to work until all the hormones already manufactured in the dog's body are exhausted; but even after three weeks most owners note a difference. The normal male dog shows no interest in a bitch not on heat, and only cursory interest in a bitch on heat for her first week; he shows no interest in mounting other male dogs, furniture or people's legs and will leave smells and lamp posts alone when trained in obedience. He is seldom a fighter.

There have been dogs that are

unstable because they are herm-aphrodite, i.e. they have two sexes in one body. This causes dogs to be bad-tempered and unreliable, as are the male dogs known as monorchids or cryptorchids. This means they have only one or neither of their two testicles descended into the scrotum. Castration in these cases is difficult and a major operation. In normal cases it is a simple and uneventful operation done by an experienced vet; no stitches need be inserted and the dog can return home in under 24 hours. The dog's mind is not adversely affected by castration. There must be no ideas in the owner's mind about denying the dog his natural pleasures; an ordinary dog doesn't get those 'natural pleasures' unless he is a stud dog or belongs to a bad owner who allows him to wander and have promiscuous relations with any bitch he meets. Dogs who have no desires don't fret because they have lost these desires; they love their owners more dearly; they are gay, happy dogs, not deluded miseries cursed by too many hormones.

After all, sex in a dog cannot be looked upon in the same way as sex in humans. Dogs don't have sex hormones for any other reason than to perpetuate the race and, with this object in mind, will get thin and miserable when a bitch is on heat in the neighbourhood; will travel miles, making their feet sore, in spite of hunger and thirst, to wait hopelessly outside a bitch's home; will take even a beating without noticing it in the attempt to attack or carry out sex impulses with other male dogs; and will destroy floors or furniture and fittings in sexual frustration. The mind of a dog doesn't look into the future if his sex

organs are to be removed; he doesn't anticipate a loss of pleasure; he has a general anaesthetic so knows nothing about the operation. Three or four days later nobody would know the dog had had anything done, except that he remains the same gay dog he always was and becomes more interested in the odd snack between meals!

With bitches this oversexed characteristic doesn't exist; the spaying of bitches, except in case of disease, is not to be lightly recommended from my experience. It is a more serious operation than castration; the bitch does become less lively, and there is a tendency to get fat. This does not mean that I think every bitch should breed a litter for her health. I think that utterly wrong. It has been proved in veterinary circles that bitches bred with are more susceptible to uterine disease than those not bred with. Many over-sentimental people worry when their pets, obviously keen to get with a dog, fret a bit and, although puppies are not wanted, they mate the bitch 'for her own sake, bless her.' I think they are wrong. There are too many unwanted dogs in this country today to warrant breeding for this reason.

Only bitches and dogs with some special points should be bred with and never if temperament is bad. Breeding will not make a bad-tempered or shy bitch or dog better tempered or non-shy; all that is being done is passing on to unfortunate dog owners a bad-tempered dog. This particularly applies to owners of breeds whose tempera-ment is deteriorating in so many cases. If a dog is mentally unhappy with his sex and shows it by fussing at all times about other dogs, castrate him. You are being kind, not cruel, to the dog and all who meet him. No psychiatrist can help the dog by mind reading. Sex is above all that nonsense. Firm training can do a lot, but take an experienced trainer's advice. No dog-loving trainer will tell you your dog is oversexed if he only lacks training.

Chapter Four

MUTUAL UNDERSTANDING

Animals are accustomed to taking commands from their herd or pack leader, and in many cases this instinct is the one that exists between master and dog, the master being the substitute for the leader. But it is not the only possibility, for I think animals can evidence a much purer love than that; and to me their wishes are solely governed by their love and respect for their owner, respect that comes from being properly trained and taught to obey necessary commands, and by so doing making it possible to live in close contact with their owner. A horse that shares its master's work or play, or lives with him for long hours as mine did in the Argentine, and is talked to and treated with sympathy and love, must develop a higher intelligence and faithfulness than one that is treated as though it were just a bicycle. People ask if the breathing up the nose has the same effect on a dog as it does on a horse? Of course it has not, because dogs know friend or foe by scent. Practically everything in a dog's life is governed primarily by this instinct. We humans all have very distinctive scents

for good or ill, and dogs know instantly whether to love you or not as they sniff at your hand or shoe. I always allow a dog to sniff me before making any approach to him; then, having been accepted, I gain his respect by being firm in my commands, exciting in the tone of voice I use if I want him to be interested, or soft and sympathetic if he is nervous. I know he must sense the great love I have for all dogs, and I caress him with extreme gentleness, using more of a smoothing gesture than a pat. I always gently scratch the chest of a new dog friend, or if I wish to praise a dog, and it has a most soothing effect.

I believe one has to give a great deal of oneself to animals if one is to get the best out of them. And, what is more, one has to treat them as one would like to be treated oneself If we are to get the best out of our dogs, it is no good shutting them up in kennels for the greater part of their lives, and then expecting them to be intelligent when they come out. In my opinion animals must live with one constantly, and learn words and thoughts that one says and

A dog must be constantly with its owner to become highly intelligent.

transmits, if they are to be true companions. I never order my dog to do things, I just ask her if she would like to shut the door for her mistress, or do whatever I want, and she instantly complies with evident pleasure. With horses I think the affection and natural obedience they have for us humans is more selfless than are the dog's. After all, a horse gets little else beyond attention to its daily needs, and being occasionally talked to and ridden, but a dog shares (if he has a good home) all the ups and down of the life of the household. By being particularly enchanting in his ways he often gets a titbit, or a game of ball, or an exciting walk, and he well knows how to melt his owner's heart. How often have I, even when really ill, staggered out onto the common for the dog's walk rather than let those beautiful brown eyes see that I don't really want to go. I always feel that, as far as is humanly possible, animals should never be let down, if one

is to have their whole-hearted affection. The dog that never knows at what time he is to go for a walk or have his meal, searches for his pleasure elsewhere. All animals live by clockwork timing; if fed regularly, their saliva starts to run at the appointed mealtime and one hardly needs a clock to live by. You should just hear the plaintive noise my cows make if I am late for milking, and the look of sad reproach they give me as I arrive! If I am early, and in a hurry, they will then hold back their milk and pay me out by going down in yield. Animals certainly give one enormous pleasure, but one tends to become a slave to them, and one's life has to be ruled according to their needs.

Praise is very important when training a dog, but this has to be done in the right way in order to make the dog feel happy with obeying you. Many people rub their dogs when praising them, and this, I know for certain, makes dogs bad-tempered. At a class once I saw a

A dog will do anything to please the owner it loves and respects.

boy rubbing his dog when I gave the command at the end of the exercise they were doing, 'Praise your dog'. I went up to him and rubbed his hair and asked him how he liked it. He went very red in the face and said he didn't like it at all, in fact he felt like 'bashing me one'. Well, if he felt like 'bashing me one' what does his dog feel like? Yet if his dog did anything like growling or biting, it would be severely reprimanded for no fault of its own. The rubbing of the hair the wrong way is particularly obnoxious to a dog, whereas the gentle smoothing of the hair on the chest or on the rumps is particularly pleasing to the dog. They love being scratched on top of the tail; it is an area of pleasure. There are many areas of pleasure – behind the ear, under the lower jaw, on the ribs behind the front legs, on the tummy and especially between the front legs. Owners must find out which pleases each individual dog best and keep that pleasure for a reward, as well as to please the dog.

Talking to Animals isn't a matter of words used, it is a matter of your thoughts, your expression, and above all the tone of your voice. A harsh voice from me can make my cows jump in terror. I shouted at old Queenie once and she got such a shock that she fell down just as if she had been shot, making me very ashamed of myself – but animals can be annoying sometimes! A horse doesn't need the harsh words 'get over' in the stable; a whispered command is all it wants. A horse's hearing is very acute and I, for one, never speak to a horse in anything but a whisper, or my 'little voice' that I keep for animals or tiny babies. Should a horse deliberately disobey, then a harsh voice should be sufficient to put terror into his mind to prevent him from repeating his offence. When I speak of 'expression' I really do mean that animals watch to see whether one's face is smiling or dull. If I don't smile at my dog, whilst she is working in the obedience tests, she fails hopelessly, just as when training her I used to look sad when she did wrong, and that hurt her. Incidentally, it is quite funny to see her

face sometimes, for she has learnt to smile by wrinkling up her eyes exactly as I do – on the other hand my daughter's little dog smiles properly by showing all her teeth. Dogs copy their owners, and perhaps that is why people say we become like our dogs.

One of the wonderful things about a dog, it seems to me, is that he never bears a grudge if one gets angry, and a kind word is enough to make the dog rapturously happy again. Human beings so often sulk for days if one has offended them. I remember some years back going to see an old farmer, and his wife said he was out in the cowshed, but ought to have been in by now. I went out to find him, and there he was fast asleep with his bucket still under the cow, his head resting gently on the cow's flank, and she in her patient way keeping quite still chewing her cud. I don't know how long he would have stayed there if I hadn't turned up, but I wondered whether it was the quest for peace, perfect peace, away from his overbearing wife, that made him seek refuge and a rest with his beloved animals. I find that my own visits to my cows and horses also always have a soothing effect on me. One has to move and speak gently when one is with animals and doing that naturally makes one relax.

Chapter Five

TRAINING TARGETS

When I am working with a class of owners and their dogs I always stress to the owners how important it is to communicate good, positive feelings towards their dogs. I explain that I worship dogs, that I have no inhibitions when I work dogs. I say silly, lovely things to them, I love them so much I can hardly keep my hands or face away from them in caress, and the problem of training them hardly ever arises for more than a few moments when we decide between ourselves who is to be master – and it most certainly is going to be me. After that it is purely a matter of showing the dog what is wanted in order to get loving and instant obedience from him. But if the owner likes to come with the dog, and honestly wishes to train him, then by copying everything I do, however silly they may think it, they have reasonable hope of having a good dog in a very short time.

I always hope that people bringing their dog for training will do so in the same frame of mind as they bring their children to the dentist or doctor, realising that to train a dog well and quickly needs one hundred per cent co-operation between dog owner and trainer. There may be a few bad trainers to whom training is only exploiting their ego or their business acumen, but most trainers are real dog lovers to whom training is a calling. Few owners realise that the training of dogs, if done conscientiously, is quite a dangerous occupation for the trainer and that, if they are bitten badly many times, it could lead to a lack of confidence in dogs which would be fatal for any trainer's work. Therefore the owner should want the dog to like the trainer and not be cross if he shows pleasure on being handled by the trainer. The owner should realise the association is only for a very short time and for the sole object of making owner and dog happy together. If this work can be done with the dog supremely happy in learning his lessons, it is nicer for the dog, although the owner naturally doesn't like sharing her dog's affection with a stranger.

Some years ago I tried out an experiment. I asked through the Press for twenty-five of the worst dogs in Britain to take part in the first

A classful of 'difficult' dogs being trained the Woodhouse way.

residential course for dogs and owners ever to be held in Britain. I wanted to prove myself right or wrong in the assumption that dogs can be trained to a high standard of obedience in a few hours. The dogs turned up with their owners; they were not all bad dogs, but a large majority were fighters, biters, pullers, won't come when called, etc. The owners hadn't all the right voices, or temperaments. Many of them found the strenuous work almost beyond them; all admitted they had no idea there was so much to learn. At the end of three days when there was nothing more I could teach them, dogs and owners passed a stiff test. There was only one failure, a German Shepherd who behaved perfectly without his owner, but who would go for people if they went too near his mistress when they were together. This guarding instinct in dogs can be dangerous, and no amount of training will stop it, unless the owner really wants to stop it, and shows great displeasure when the dog attacks. Most owners of this type of dog had grown to like being well protected. But once the instinct has been developed to this extent, the dog, in my opinion, is unreliable and therefore dangerous. Away from its owner the

German Shepherd was trained to a high standard and was sweet-tempered.

Most women, to begin with, think the training is harsh, and find it difficult to jerk their dogs, or put them to the 'down' position. Unless they can master this over-sentimental feeling they will fail. If you learn the correct way of doing these things it is akin to jujitsu and in no way hurts or upsets the dog. The slow way on the other hand annoys the dog and often leads to bites. The best dog handler is the quick-minded type of person who wants to learn it all in a day. To those who say you must walk before you run in dog training, I say: 'Nonsense': if you can keep up with your dog's brain there is no need to worry. I have no hesitation in saying it is inevitably the owner who is much slower to learn than the dog; and they admit it.

Very often one has to train the dog who in turn trains the owner. I have often seen a dog, on my command: 'Halt', sit, whilst the owner has absentmindedly walked on, only to be brought to a standstill by the dog. The question of age of the dog constantly crops up. Are there limits as to when one can train a dog? My answer is: any age between three months and eight years old, providing the dog is fit. After that the dog in my opinion should not be bothered by training; before that the puppy gets tired too quickly. The age of the owner matters far more. Training a dog is almost a gymnastic feat in my classes. The owner has to bend down quickly to push her dog to the sit many times in an hour. Speed in working is essential if you want your dog to work happily. Dawdlers make bad handlers. If you want your dog to walk well to heel don't wait for it; stride out, and if it doesn't keep up, jerk it quickly on and up to you using an excited tone of voice and lots of praise. The slower you go the slower the dog will go, and the more bored you both will be. Running and stopping suddenly teaches a dog to sit like lightning and becomes quite a game. No room here for twenty stone of fat. Dog training revitalises owners, if done in the right spirit with others in a class, and it can be wonderful fun at home when you feel like making progress. If you feel irritable or worried don't train your dog. Train him when you and he are in a happy mood; get quick results; give quick praise, and then leave him in peace. Never nag. What can't be achieved in ten minutes will seldom be achieved in ten hours of boredom for the dog.

Some owners choose big dogs and do not have the physical strength to control them or train them. Unless these breeds are trained young, few women can do anything with them. Breeds like Pyrenean Mountain Dogs and Boxers come into this category, for they have enormous strength and will-power when adult. Providing they get the right type of owners there are few dogs which cannot be made into reasonable companions. But I regret to say that there are a vast number of misfits in this dog-owner partnership. With some I believe it is a sheer waste of time attempting to train them. The most difficult to help are the elderly owners, either man or woman, who for purely physical reasons cannot carry out the necessary corrections. Many of them have arthritis in their joints, which makes them weak in the wrists, or makes bending down to put the dog to

Breeds such as Pyrenean Mountain Dogs and Boxers have tremendous will-power and strength when they are full grown.

the sit almost an impossibility. Yet they love their dogs and are often the keenest of learners.

Is it fair that they should have to put up with disobedient dogs, or is there some way of helping them train their dogs? Yes, there is. For example, when teaching a dog to lie down I usually use two methods. In one I put the dog to the sit, and standing in front of it, I lift one leg and push the opposite shoulder, which puts the dog off its balance and down it goes without fuss. Or when walking I catch hold of the running end of the choke chain underneath the chin and pull it quickly to the ground slightly ahead of the dog's chin. Then a quick press on the dog's flank with the other hand completes the movement and down goes the dog, again without fuss if done swiftly enough. Now it is quite obvious that these exercises could not be easily carried out by elderly or infirm people. Yet this 'down' exercise is wanted for the cure of almost every vice, for at the 'down' you have your dog under your control. Well, this exercise can be done just as easily by placing the left foot over the lead when you are standing up so that the lead runs under the arch of your shoe. Then pull quickly and strongly on the lead, and the dog's head is pulled to the down, and it quickly lies down to get more comfortable.

To teach a dog to sit on command it is not necessary to use the left hand to push the dog down. It can just as well be done by working the dog against a wall on the left-hand side so that he cannot sidle away from you, and then with the firm command: "Sit" give the dog's rump a tap with a rolled-up newspaper or the end of another leather lead which you have in your hand. It is the noise that makes the dog sit, not any pain caused by the tap. If the dog shows signs of biting, as some nasty dogs do when put to the down, muzzle them for one or two minutes; they will soon find out that they cannot bite and must go down, and that directly they have gone into the down position they get praise, and then all idea of biting in retaliation will be given up. Be sure when making a dog sit that the lead, which is always held in the right hand for training purposes, is raised tightly over the right hip, for that almost puts a dog in the sitting position without further help.

Pulling on the lead can seldom be cured by infirm people because the dog needs a really quick sharp jerk to correct him. It is for this reason that I do not recommend big dogs or heavy boisterous dogs for old people. Even if they get some young person, or the trainer at a club, to do the initial pulling, the dog will soon realize he has his elderly owner at his mercy and will start pulling again. One thing can be done, however. Take the dog's lead in your left hand and whilst walking with it, turn sharply, throwing the right leg in front of the dog's nose and turning to the left all the time. The dog is checked quickly because otherwise he would bump into that right leg and he won't bump into the leg more than once or twice before he realises it is safer to keep back. Always use the word 'heel' as you turn. Association of ideas lies beneath the whole system of training: that, and the praise the dog gets when he does right.

I cannot stress too strongly that an owner who is frightened of his dog must protect himself if he wishes to train the

Putting a dog in the 'down' is a cure for almost every vice.

For the elderly or infirm the 'down' can be achieved by standing on the lead with your left foot when you are standing up, and then pulling quickly and strongly with the lead.

animal. If you know your dog will bite when you try to make him lie down, naturally you are sending out fear waves, and the dog knows you are beaten and will bite all the more. If however you have protected your hands by thick leather gloves, you can with confidence ignore the efforts of the dog to bite, and what is better, retaliate with two or three good jerks on his choke chain. Unfortunately nobody can teach your dog to respect you. They can teach the dog the exercise, so that he knows what to do, but you yourself must carry out that exercise with confidence, secure in the knowledge that the dog cannot hurt you. Then and only then will the dog obey you happily. As soon as the dog obeys, cast away your protection, and have confidence

Putting a dog in the 'sit': place left hand over dog's left hip.

Keep your thumb towards your own leg; do not exert pressure on the dog's back.

that you will not be bitten. Directly the dog has been put down, scratch his chest, for no dog will bite when you are scratching his chest, it is a movement that calms the fiercest breast.

I don't believe timid people make good trainers. I don't believe over-sentimental people make good trainers, as with any problem dog there is bound to be friction at one time or another until the dog recognises who is master. If you feel quite sick at having to jerk a dog on its choke chain you will not do it with vigour, you will therefore nag at the dog with ineffectual jerks which would never train a dog, and both you and he are getting nowhere. If you take a dog to a training school undoubtedly you get help. I do all the initial jerks necessary to save the owner and the dog from misunderstandings, but the owner must keep up to the high standard reached in class when the class is over. If you do not, the dog becomes cunning and behaves like a lamb in class, only to throw off the cloak of goodness later on.

I well remember a lady who had just won the obedience certificate at a dog show being pulled like nothing on earth down the street, shouting at me as she passed at her dog's speed, 'What price my future obedience champion?' Personally I wouldn't have tolerated such behaviour, but she thought it funny. And that brings me to another aspect of training dogs. So many people think their naughty dogs are really rather funny. If they think that, there is no hope for them or their dogs, as they do not really object to the dog's faults. You must really want to make your dog good, you must put everything you have got into teaching him kindly

but quickly to obey. If one day you rock with laughter at his having eaten your knitting, and roar with rage the next day when it is your Sunday hat, how is the dog to know what you will tolerate and what you won't? I don't tolerate destruction of any kind; if one day you allow him to play with your old gloves, how is he to know the difference when he finds your new gloves and tears them up?

Quite the most difficult thing to teach owners is enthusiasm. How dry and dull I find lots of them; they don't seem to be terribly pleased when the dog does right, it doesn't seem to matter much when the dog does wrong, and the result is a sort of grey picture with no light or shade. The dog also becomes grey in nature, he does his training with his tail down, he yawns as he stays resignedly at the 'sit' or 'down', and eventually herefuses to do anything well – he is happy in his mediocrity. I hate that; I like to appear very angry when the dog does wrong, although curiously enough I never feel angry with the dogs. I like to bubble over with joy when they do right. I know I must look a perfect ass when training dogs – a cross between a ballet dancer and a clown – for I am always on the move. I try not to let the dogs feel bored for a second whilst that particular exercise is being carried out, and I always have a quick romp with each one after every exercise. I shall be sorry when I become too old to feel like this, for in spite of the fact that one pupil remarked that my classes were more like the Palladium than a dog class, I do believe that enthusiasm in working both dogs and owners is essential for success.

One of the most difficult things I have

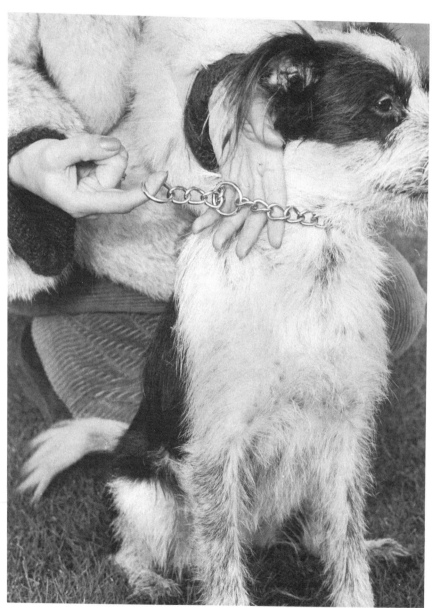

When a choke chain is put on correctly, it automatically loosens after it has been jerked by the owner.

to cope with very often is getting a depressed dog's tail up, and making the dog happy not only in ordinary life but for the show ring too. This, to many of the exhibitors is something that completely defeats them, and the depression the owner feels at seeing the dog's tail down between the legs is passed to the dog, and so the trouble never ends. Many dogs hate dog shows, and I think if a dog really hates every second of the show business, he will never win the highest honours whatever his beauty and conformation. For it is the out-going happy character that adds to the beauty of any show dog. I think in the first place the dogs must be taught that this show business is not meant to be just fun. It is meant to be a lesson to be learnt and that when it is all over, fun will be the reward. That is why I hate 'ringcraft' classes, for who is to teach a lot of breeds of dogs with different temperaments ringcraft? many depressed dogs have suffered from this type of training. I think it is better for the owner to go to several shows by herself and watch the experts at work, and then go home and practise – for short spells at a time – the handling that appears to win the major prizes. Professional handlers so often win the top prizes because they instil confidence in their dogs, whilst the owners do not instil confidence in their dogs. Everyone wants to win so much that I think even the most hardened of exhibitors must feel nervous when showing their own dogs. The professional handler has supreme confidence and has trained the dog by his own technique to the required standard, yet I would much rather see an owner get to the top with her own efforts.

Tails drop into the misery stance between the legs for many reasons: the dog is unsure of the owner's wishes, the dog is bored, the dog is frightened, the dog is tired. All these things must be eliminated if the dog's tail is to assume its correct height. Tails can be made to stay upright in the case of Pekes, Chihuahuas, Papillons and Poms etc. by brushing your hand with the lightest possible touch from the base of the tail to the tip in a very fast flick movement. This gives out static electricity and the tail stays up for the short time the judge is looking at the dog. Eventually the dog so likes the flick movement that the tail stays up. But the quickest way too start the tail coming from between the dog's legs is to run really fast giving quick jerks on the choke chain. The dog's tail is there to balance it, the jerks unbalance it and the tail rises to counteract the unbalancing motion. In time, as you get ready to run with the dog it is so used to being unbalanced by the jerks that it holds its tail up form the beginning, in case the owner intends jerking. Dogs are very quick to learn.

The best way is, of course, happiness to make a dog hold his tail in the correct manner, and this happiness only stems form the owner's treatment of the dog. Is he getting enough doggy pursuits? Does he look forward with happy anticipation to an outing with the owner? Or is he accustomed to a miserable walk around the block without ever the fun of ever being free to to play and romp with other dogs. Is he taught lots of new things and given lots of praise? A clever dog is seldom a depressed dog. Try bringing a show dog with tail trouble into your home and teaching him things. Cultivate an

When a dog is working and happy it will hold its tail at half-mast.

interesting tone of voice. I taught my dogs police work and when at shows, I only had to use the voice that meant we were going to chase a criminal to make their ears alert, and the dog's whole attitude one of excited expectancy. This was when the dog looked his best, and his attention was on the direction I had initially pointed to. Nerves seem to be the most usual cause of tails between legs. Nerves can be cured in a very short time. When the dog is no longer afraid he naturally holds his tail in the happy position. Sentimental owners will never cure nerves, for nerves can only be cured by confident owners.

How I hate to see dogs and owners ploughing round a hall with the trainer issuing orders which many owners don't comprehend or carry out. How I hate the idea that if a dog fails on something he cannot have another chance because of shortage of time. That is why I find my weekend courses so satisfying. I have all day to cure the dogs' and owners' faults, no one grumbles if I spend twenty minutes on one dog and then win, for that is what we are there for – to make sure no dog leaves with the faults he came with. I think they are as anxious as I am that the dog should be good. There is a great camaraderie amongst owners of difficult dogs, and if we all pull together we must win. So often in the street I feel like snatching a pulling dog from his owner, correcting him, and giving him back. One day I was walking behind a very troublesome dog, and I heard the owner say: "If you don't behave I shall take you to Mrs Woodhouse." I never let on that the threat could easily have been carried out sooner than the dog anticipated!

Sometimes the training or correction of the dog in the home is impossible because the husband or wife or some other relative doesn't approve of the training and deliberately spoils the dog, or lets the dog get away with doing wrong because he thinks it cruel to train dogs, or rather enjoys seeing the dog do naughty things in the same way as: 'Boys will be boys'. Then there is the opposite type who imagines himself a smashing dog trainer. He doesn't need anyone to show him what to do, he thunders at the dog, gets poor results, then out of pique suggests the best cure for naughty dogs is to sell them, give them away or put them down. This causes great rifts in families, and I shudder to think of the number of divorces or quarrels dogs have caused in the past. I well remember the husband of one person I met who had shouted at her: "Get rid of that dog or I go." "That is easily answered," said the wife, "go". Many a quarrel is caused by differences of opinion as to whether the dog shall live in the house or a kennel. Whether the dog shall sleep on the bed or in his basket. Whether the wife can accompany the husband on an outing where dogs cannot go. All these rows could be avoided if the dog were trained, for a trained dog does not need a baby sitter, a trained dog sleeps in his own bed, a trained dog makes no mess or trouble in a house, so the kennel plan never comes into operation.

What a joy it is to meet some of the people who train their dogs intelligently and who endeavour, with help, to follow instructions; who practise their dogs at home, and are rewarded by owning a delightful and obedient pal who can be taken anywhere without a preliminary working-out of the snags. Man's life is made richer by owning a dog, but the enrichment is vastly increased if he owns a well-trained, healthy, clean and intelligent one.

Chapter Six

TALKING TO ANIMALS

Most dogs can be trained if spoken to gently and quietly, but with many, much difference in intonation must be used before they will listen and obey. I think I know how to use all the different intonations needed to attract a dog's attention, and to make him obey a command, and he seems to love my 'little voice' that I use to caress him at the end. It is an intriguing sight – and a rather embarrassing one – when my class of dogs and owners have finished an exercise, to find the dogs deserting their owners and coming to me for praise. I think the explanation of this lies in my own pleasure in their performance. The same thing happens when, in an exercise, we are trying to make a dog walk nicely to heel, for nine times out of ten he will wander away from his owner. Perhaps this is because the owner tends to let his voice sound dull. So I tell them to use a more exciting tone, as if there were rats to be found everywhere – but I seldom get the voice I want, alas.

I spend many hours teaching tone of voice to the owners, and we had a film made at a course which clearly shows the response by the dogs to the owners' tone of voice, and then my voice. Inevitably some of the dogs came to me, not the owners, but it was fascinating to watch the steady improvement in the owners; to see them learn to let themselves go with praise when the dogs obeyed, and steadily learn to use the right firm tone in giving commands, and thus getting instant obedience. Bit by bit they got accustomed to the fact that to give a dog a very sharp jerk on a choke chain is not cruel. In fact the dogs who were depressed cheered up as soon as I jerked them firmly and confidently, secure in the knowledge that the right choke chain could not hurt them. This I demonstrated on my own wrist. Whilst I am on the subject of choke chains, far, far too many people have the wrong type. They buy the thin ones in the mistaken idea that they are kinder than the thick ones. I refuse to work a dog on a thin one, as I know it hurts the dog. I feel quite sure that the wrong chain retards the dog's progress.

I train many hundreds of owners in a year, and it depresses me how dull and

Enthusiasm is catching and owners must make training seem like fun.

flat in voice and spirit many of them are. First of all remember that a dog cannot concentrate for a great length of time, so when you are training him, do so only in short spells. Speak in an excited, keen voice; give really hard jerks on the choke chain, not half-hearted ones. Praise with joy in your voice and laughter in your eyes, in fact, try to have that little extra something that makes a dog want your love and appreciation. If you move slowly, give commands in a dull, slow voice, and don't mind terribly whether the dog does the exercise very well or not, you will never have a dog that is interested in his work. Enthusiasm is catching, whether you are dealing with dogs or with human beings. If the dog does wrong, shake him or jerk him hard on the choke chain. After that he will watch your every movement, waiting for

the return of your loving mood. The dog will be thrilled if you praise him when he does what you want. So few people have the power of making everything in work or play seem fun. I suppose their home lives aren't terribly interesting. Unfortunately dogs mirror their owners and a dull owner makes a dull, uninterested dog. Cultivate pep, and your dog will be enchanted with your every command.

What do I do if the owner cannot get the right tone of voice? That is one of my big problems; it is a physical impossibility for many women to have a wide range of tone. If they try to get the right tone it often ends up as a squeak. This makes training doubly difficult for those people. All they can do is to train their dogs by voice and signal, and eventually work almost entirely on signal. The tone of voice coupled with

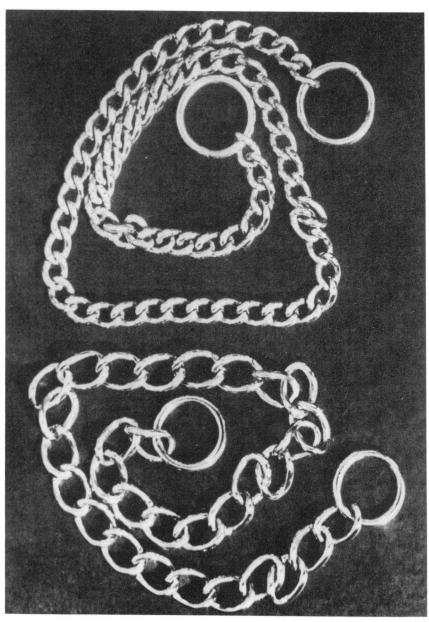

Choke chains: The broader the link, the kinder to the dog.

Cultivate 'pep' and the dog will be enchanted with your every command.

sending out the right telepathic thought is most important. You would be surprised how dogs pick up thought before you have ever said a word. It is useless giving commands without willing them to obey with your mind as well.

The importance of your tone of voice when speaking to animals (or human beings for that matter) was made very clear to me when I was in Gambia a few years back. I went to the Abuco rain forests where the nature reserves are. In a cage was a hyena which had continued, ever since its captivity, to throw itself from one end of it to another, hoping to escape. Nothing could persuade it to stop in its misery and fear. I asked the keeper if he would allow me to go and talk to the hyena. He said I could, so I went over to it, and in what I call my 'little voice' (which is a fairly soft high-pitched tone) I said; "Come along, come along." It stopped throwing itself against the cage and came up to me. It raised its nose to mine, put its ear flat against its face in what I call the 'soft look' which means that the animals welcomes you and, actually wriggled as it came up to me, laid its head against my chest and breathed up my nose. Then it lay down at my feet. I was so amazed at the reaction of this animal that I asked the keeper if I could get out to the reserve where there were many more hyenas, and he said I could. I was not allowed in with them, so I stayed outside the wire and again used my 'little voice' to call them, which incidentally, my mother always asked me to use in the old days if there was an unhappy dog in the boarding kennels. She would say: "Go and talk to the dog, Barbara in your 'little voice' – it always makes them happy." Well, I called the hyenas, and one by one, they all came back to me, laying their heads as near to mine as they could and breathing up my nose. One got near enough to push up the wire and lay its head on my chest, and then the whole lot came up, breathed up my nose and laid down at my feet.

Later on that day I went with an expedition to a big resevoir, which was very beautiful. I was standing on some concrete when a praying mantis ran out. I had never seen one before; it looked like a locust to me, but green, rather like an enormous grasshopper. It was terrified of all the tourists and raced about, so I said jokingly to them: "If you stand still, I will train it for you." I managed to get within a few inches of it and told it to "sit and stay" with the sit and stay signal I use for dogs. It looked at me, stopping in its tracks. I then said "Lift up your feet. Higher, come on. Sit up," because I knew that praying mantises sit on their hindlegs. It lifted its feet up and I said: "No, higher." We got some perfect photographs of this strange creature obeying my commands with its feet lifted high in the air. Then I was asked to put it in a white coat as it would photograph better, so I picked it up. It had no fear and again, it obeyed me and sat up bringing its feet up. The tourists finished taking their pictures. I then told the mantis to "hop it" and off it went. I was as surprised as the tourists were to its response to my commands and tone of voice.

I have lots of photographs of dogs watching the television series I did, and their owners believed their dogs were responding to my voice and to my commands. We therefore tried an experiment; I was ten miles away with outside broadcast cameras, and the dog I was to train was ten miles away in the studio. The dog heard my voice, saw me on the screen in the studio, and after peering round the television set to see where I was, obeyed all my commands instantly. Another instance which stays clearly in my mind dates back to much earlier days. I remember I was at Oxford by the river, and on the other side of the bank stood a man with his German Shepherd. Well, I have always been very fond of German Shepherds, and I called out: "Hello, boy", in a nice bright voice. The dog immediately plunged into the river and came over to me. I apologised to the owner, and said that I never could resist talking to a German Shepherd. He replied that he had never seen his dog go to anyone else in his life. I explained that I thought it was my tone of voice, and suggested that I called the dog again. The owner assured me that the dog would not come a second time, and

I bet him five pounds that the dog would! The man agreed, and so I called the dog back again. It instantly plunged straight into the river and came to me. Unfortunately the man was on the other side so I could not collect my five pounds!

I believe that by being constantly with their owners, by listening to conversation, and by connecting certain sounds with certain actions, the dog can and does understand about four hundred words, more if it is a well-loved, extremely intelligent dog. Dogs work out for themselves how to avoid scoldings for wrong-doing, how to get what they want without the owner meaning to give it to them by being particularly winning in their ways. They know when to sympathise with their owners by a gentle contact of the muzzle with the owners' hand or knee, and that look of adoration in their eyes. Dogs may not be human, but some are not far off in intelligence.

Chapter Seven

TELEPATHIC POWERS

I have hundreds of letters from animal lovers all over the world asking me to tell them more about this business of 'talking to animals'. They want to know whether, if shown how to do it, others, apart from myself, can communicate with their pets so that they truly understand. They want to know whether the breathing down my nose that I practise with horses works with dogs. Someone even wanted to know whether I agreed with his theory that we all get the animals we deserve. I don't believe that on being shown how to do it everyone can actually communicate with animals in the same way as I do myself. There is much more to it than that: first and foremost I think one has to have a very deep love for all the animals one comes in contact with, and coupled with that one must be without fear. There is nothing so catching as fear; animals can pick up fear at quite a distance away, and their hearing is far more acute than a human being's. Think how rabbits all go to their burrows at a thump from the buck's foot as a warning of danger, and how the stamp of a horse's foot, and a snort,

will raise every head in the wild horse herd and cause the foals to gallop about in fear. But things even less perceptible to us than small sounds can make animals frightened.

They seem to me to pick up fear as a fear-thought enters the mind of the person dealing with them. That is why horses refuse jumps. The question as to whether they will do it or not has entered the rider's mind and been flashed to the horse's brain. With someone who has complete confidence that the horse can and will get over the obstacle, this does not occur, unless the animal has grown cunning or is sick of jumping. In this book I am not of course talking of wicked or cunning animals — like wicked people, they need different treatment.

I am absolutely certain that people send out waves of love or confidence, fear or hate, according to their circumstances, and that animals are accustomed to this kind of communication between themselves, and it is quite hopeless to try to fool an animal. I have often seen people trying apparently to make their dogs do

A dog will pick up its owner's moods, sensing love, fear or happiness.

something, while in their innermost hearts they thought it unnecessary, or too hard, or even perhaps silly. They tell me the dog won't do it, but I tell them I know the dog will do what they ask, provided that they are certain of it in their minds. I then take their dog myself and get it to do the exercise at once. I am quite sure that the animal picks up my trust and confidence in his good behaviour and immediately wants to please.

With horses and cattle it is the same. When I breathe down my nose to say how do you do to a horse, It can hear that breath at anything up to twenty yards, for horses have the most acute sense of hearing. I always teach my horses in a whisper all the commands that are necessary, and after I have breathed my first welcome to them I find they have no fear. Then the love I have for them is transmitted through my fingers. My touch soothes them and often I have seen them shut their eyes in contentment. Horses know in exactly the same way whether you have confidence in them, and a nervous rider can ruin a top-class jumper for many a day. Often a horse starts shying because the rider sees something rather terrifying ahead and instinctively tightens the hold on the reins or the knee grip, or even just transmits fear by telepathy; with a confident rider the horse probably would have not shied, or only have shied very little. That is why I say my method of breathing up a horse's nose would not work for everyone as a foolproof method for breaking in horses. Many people don't believe in it anyway, and therefore their chances of success are practically nil. Others would like to believe, but can't

be sure; their chances are also doubtful, for the horse will sense the doubt in their minds. Others go about it too quickly, in the firm belief that there is nothing in breaking in a horse anyway; they are what I term the 'commando' type, and horses don't like that sort of approach. I believe that this breathing removes fear, but you must not give the horse any reason to become afraid again; so it is still necessary to move firmly but gently, to speak softly, and to have abundant patience in just showing your very willing friend what he must do.

When communicating with a dog it is important to understand what means a dog has of understanding and reasoning. It has a well-developed brain, it has an acute sense of hearing. It has first-class eyesight; they can see prey almost imperceptibly in the undergrowth, and it has a very acute sense of smell. Added to all these it has a first-class memory, which includes a guilty conscience. It has instinct and indisputable psychic powers; how else could a dog know when its owner's car and its beloved owner were approaching but still some miles away, or sense the impending departure of its owner? All these things – and a lot more – no one in their senses disputes, for the evidence in favour is overwelming. Therefore, when owners say of beloved dogs that they understand every word that is said to them, I think they mean not so much individual words but meaning of sounds. The meaning of words is conveyed to a dog by the tone of voice and by scent from the owner; sweat for example, has a strong smell which often conveys fear to a dog. Association of ideas is well known in the dog world, and it is by this method we train dogs. We teach them what makes us pleased so that they get praise and love, and what makes us displeased. They learn to recognise noises of dinner time, they pick up their owner's thoughts about whether to take the dog for a walk or not, and owners then think is is the word 'walkies' that the dog understands. Undoubtedly it does understand the word, but it has also understood the thought, and I believe that if the owner said "carrots" in the same tone of voice used usually for walks, the dog would get the interpretation. Once I was driving down our common and my dog was five hundred yards behind the car sniffing and taking her time to come on, as I allow on these occasions. Suddenly I thought I might turn up a parallel road and go back. I did or said nothing, I only thought about it, yet my dog stopped expectantly at that turning. She had picked up my thought five hundred yards away without any other indication of what I was going to do. Explain that away if you can.

Haven't you often noticed that a word of praise goes much further than a scolding also with human beings, and that if you have a preconceived idea that a person is nice, nine times out of ten that person will be? That is how I feel about the bad dogs that are brought to me. I blame the owners' temperaments or methods of handling, for I believe that the dog is fundamentally a well-meaning fellow. A rather good example of this recently was a large Bull Mastiff brought to me as absolutely impossible to brush; he bit his owner if she attempted to do it. So I took the dog on a loose lead and said to him, "Who's going to have a simply *lovely*

brushing?" in a most excited tone of voice. He looked at me expectantly, wagging his tail hard, and I went on for a few moments, telling him he really was the luckiest dog, and so forth; and then I brushed him, and he stood quite still except for the gentle tail-wagging which he kept up. When I stopped, he turned round to look at me, and I asked him if he wanted some more. The tail wagged faster, and I brushed him again, keeping up my talking to him about how lovely he was, and how lucky. The owner had suspected he might bite her, and her fear had transmitted itself to her dog until he thought brushing must be something to fear. I, on the other hand, knew the dog would not bite me, and transmitted confidence by voice, by telepathy, and by firm use of the brush.

You should always bear in mind that the dog picks up your thoughts by an acute telepathic sense, and it is useless to be thinking one thing and saying another; you cannot fool a dog. If you wish to talk to your dog you must do so with your mind and will power, as well as your voice. I communicate my wishes by my voice, my mind, and by the love I have for animals, and by caressing them with my hands. If you are 'in tune' with your dog he will work for you cheerfully and well. Never attempt to train a dog when irritable or angry; you will be sending out waves of irritability which the dog's sensitive nervous system will pick up, and he will worry all the time. Choose a time when you are placid, and looking forward to teaching your dog his useful lessons. Remember that sense and sentiment do not always go hand in hand.

Equally, it is important to try to understand when your dog doesn't perhaps feel one hundred per cent well, then you should leave out the long walk or the training for that day. Usually the eye of a dog gives away his health and his mood. When I am training, my eyes are forever watching the eyes of the dog I am training. I then know whether he intends co-operating or whether his mind is on other things. If his mind is on other things, I become much firmer with him until he realises second best is not good enough for me, or for his owner in due course. But the other side of the situation is the mind of the owner. Is he or she really concentrating on the dog's behaviour or is the mind also wandering? If so, give up training for that day, as one should do if not feeling well or in a bad mood. Dogs are very sympathetic animals if truly loved. They seem to sense when quiet sympathy is what is wanted from them and do not intrude on the owner's thoughts or actions when the owner is not in the mood. But this takes understanding from the owner and a lot of companionship with the dog, as well as talking to the dog. I wonder how many words in a day the average owner speaks to the dog. Usually it is very few. Amongst those few may be: 'Din dins, walkies, shut up, go to your bed, and good boy or girl,' but actual conversation is not all that common. I used to really talk to my dogs, whose understanding became 'almost human'.

It is extraordinary how dogs pick up praise straight from your brain almost before you have had time to put it into words. A dog's mind is so quick in picking up your thoughts that, as you think them, they enter the dog's mind simultaneously. I have great difficulty in this matter in giving the owners

commands in class for the dog obeys my thoughts before my mouth has had time to give the owner the command. I find it extremely difficult to correct a dog for this, although it shouldn't really be obeying me; it should be tuned into the owner who of course doesn't know what I am going to say until I have said it – that is unless the owner is also telepathic. In the same way I know what the dog is thinking as it thinks it, and can often therefore stop it being naughty or disobedient before it has erred, which saves correcting it and helps quick training. But I find the chattering that goes on in class by those people who don't truly concentrate very hampering to this mind communication. It is like having constant interference on a wireless set. But then I don't suppose many people know what a thrill it is to be on the same wavelength as a dog.

The mind of a dog is forever open to take in, by touch, by telepathy, and by talking, the feelings, ideas, emotions and wishes of its owner. That is, if the dog loves his owner. To get through to a dog's mind you don't need a couch and sweet music or probing questions from a psychiatrist. You need hands that on touching the dog send messages of love and sympathy to his brain. You need a voice with a wide range of tones to convey aurally your wishes and feelings towards the dog. You need eyes that tell the dog who watches them what you are feeling towards him, even though it may be hidden from the outside world, and above all you need telepathy so that the dog thinks with you. These things are not always born in people. They can be developed as any sense or gift can be developed. That is, providing the person who wishes to develop them is honest in mind, because with animals you cannot cheat; it is useless watching a trainer handling your dog with hatred of her in your heart, or dislike of all the things she is doing which you think unnecessary or harsh, or both. If you give an order to your dog by word of mouth and are feeling sorry for it inside you are doomed to failure. Dogs above all creatures love honesty of purpose. If you pat a dog and your fingers are not carrying that loving message, you don't deceive the dog.

APPENDIX

A range of other books, tapes and accessories are available to help you derive the full benefit from the Barbara Woodhouse approach to dog training.

Other titles in this series are:

Barbara Woodhouse On Handling A Problem Dog

Whether it is an aggressive dog, a nervous dog, a roaming dog or a thief, Barbara Woodhouse believes that with proper understanding, most faults can be cured quickly and a happy relationship can be built up between owner and dog. At this time, more than any other, it is essential that all dogs are well behaved and live in harmony with their owners and with society. Barbara, who has trained some 19,000 dogs, tackles a wide spectrum of 'problem dogs' and comes up with sound, commonsense solutions.

Barbara Woodhouse On Training Your Dog

Barbara guides the owner through the first steps of basic obedience, essential for the family pet, and graduates, stage by stage, to more advanced and specialised training. This book is essential for every owner who wants their dog to be "a pleasure to all, and a nuisance to none."

Barbara Woodhouse On Keeping Your Dog Healthy

In a lifetime spent boarding, breeding and training dogs, she has come across all the most common conditions and complaints affecting dogs, and she gives practical, no-nonsense advice on all aspects of dog care, from diet, exercise and grooming to breeding, diagnosing health problems and nursing a dog through a serious illness. When you buy a dog, you are responsible for all its physical and mental needs, and this book tells you all you need to know to be a firm, fair and loving owner.

Barbara Woodhouse On How To Train Your Puppy

IBarbara gives invaluable advice on house training, diet, exercise, and early training, and perhaps most important of all, she helps new owners get off to the right start, so that they can achieve a happy working relationship with their dog.

All these titles should be available through your local pet or book shop, price £3.99 each. In cases of difficulty they can be ordered direct from the publisher.
(Please add 75p per title towards P&P).
See address at the end of this section.

The Complete Woodhouse Guide To Dog Training

This is the definitive volume on dog training from Britain's best-loved expert.
Everything you need to know about the care and control of your dog; how to
understand his behaviour and how to get the best from him.
This book contains the very best of Barbara Woodhouse's writing
on a subject she understands like no other.
Available from good bookshops everywhere, price £14.95

*In case of difficulty The Complete Woodhouse Guide To Dog Training
can be ordered direct from the publisher.*
(Please add £1.50 towards P&P).
See address at the end of this section.

And if you've read the book, it is time to see the movie!

THE <u>WOODHOUSE</u> VIDEO
Barbara Woodhouse:
Quick Dog Training

A complete programme of obedience exercises for you and your dog. This 90 minute video takes you step-by-step through all the essential commands: Sit, Stay, Wait, Down, Leave and Recall.
PLUS house training, giving medicine, obedience in the car and on the street, walking to heel and much, much more from the most celebrated dog trainer in the world.

Price: £14.99
(plus £1.50 P&P)

Available ONLY from the publisher.
See address at the end of this section

BARBARA WOODHOUSE
CHOKE CHAINS AND LEADS
Are also available through the publisher

CHOKE CHAINS

Sizes at two–inch intervals
Twelve inches to eighteen inches   £3.00
Twenty inches to Twenty-eight inches   £3.50

To obtain the correct choke chain, measure over the top of the dog's
head, down over the ears and under the chin, then add two inches
and round up or down to the nearest size.
Please add 95p P&P to each order

LEADS

Approx four foot long in best quality bridle leather
Large or small trigger hooks   £5.95
Please add 95p P&P to each order

BARBARA WOODHOUSE AUDIO CASSETTE

BASED ON THE SERIES
TRAINING DOGS THE WOODHOUSE WAY
Price: £5.95
(including postage and packing)

HOW TO ORDER

All the items described here can be ordered
direct from the publisher

RINGPRESS BOOKS LTD.,
SPIRELLA HOUSE, BRIDGE ROAD,
LETCHWORTH, HERTS SG6 4ET

Please remember to add postage and packing charge where
necessary and allow 21 days for delivery.

ACCESS and VISA card holder may order by telephone on
0462 674177

Office open 9am to 5pm Monday to Friday